Night-time
2003
180 × 200 cm
oil on canvas

Partou Zia
Entering the Visionary Zone

Essay by Dr Virginia Button

A Sense of Space
Tate St Ives Artist Residency Programme

Susan Daniel McElroy and Sara Hughes

At the opening of his exhibition in Plymouth 1955, Peter Lanyon paid an affectionate tribute to a most respected friend. "If it had not been for Borlase Smart, I should never have started painting at all. .... If it hadn't been for him there would be very few artists in St Ives today."

Robert Borlase Smart, a driving force in the St Ives Society of Artists, was well remembered for his breadth of view and the encouragement he gave to the younger generation of avant-garde artists throughout the 1940s. Two years after his death in 1947, his memorial fund helped to purchase the Porthmeor Studios complex, where he had worked for nearly 30 years, to preserve them for artists' use. Latterly a resident of Studio Number 5, Smart is one of many influential artists to occupy and exhibit in a studio that has been central to the history of the St Ives School and the rise of British Modernism.

It is befitting therefore that in collaboration with the Borlase Smart, John Wells Trust, Tate St Ives has instigated a residency programme from 'Number 5' to support the development of emerging young artists, living and working in Cornwall. As well as bringing the studio back to life, the year long pilot project, split into two sixth month segments, aims to give dedicated practitioners both intellectual and physical space (this sky lit studio spans some 100 square metres) to develop their work.

My Accomplice I
2003
154 × 183 cm
oil on canvas

Partou Zia, the first artist to work on the programme, has used the time to reflect on the writing and painting of William Blake to engage with the poetics of her unconscious worlds. *Entering the Visionary Zone* is an exhibition of selected works made by Partou during March to September this year. Virginia Button's insightful essay discusses Blakean ideology in relation to the artist's inquiry and the evolutionary steps Partou has made in her work during this unique experience.

The planning and implementation of this project has been extensive. We are exceedingly grateful to the trustees of the Borlase Smart, John Wells Trust for participating in our programme.

The fundraising has also been substantial and we are grateful to the following organisations for their enthusiasm and support: The Esmee Fairbairn Foundation, Arts Council of England, South West, decibel, Tate Members and The Creative Skills Consortium. Thanks also to Falmouth College of Arts for contributing to the catalogue production costs.

We would also like to acknowledge the help and advice of the following individuals: Shreela Gosh, Zoe Li, Judith Robinson, Jennifer Cormack, Sinead McKenna, Norman Pollard, Simon Pollard and Trevor Bell.

Lastly, our warm thanks to Partou Zia for her commitment and energy throughout this project.

My Accomplice II
2003
154 × 183 cm
oil on canvas

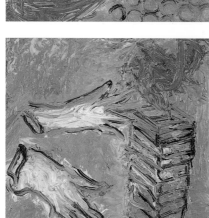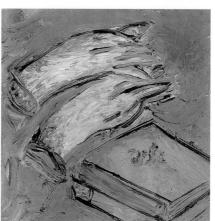

(L–R)

Red Wool
2003
30 × 30 cm
oil on canvas

Telling Yarns
2003
30 × 30 cm
oil on canvas

(L–R)

Heated Issues
2003
30 × 30 cm
oil on canvas

Hand Readings
2003
30 × 30 cm
oil on canvas

(L–R)

Green Book
2003
20.3 × 10.5 cm
oil on panel

Red Book
2003
10.8 × 10.5 cm
oil on panel

White Bowl
2003
10.8 × 10.4 cm
oil on panel

(L–R)

Red Head II
2003
23 × 10.5 cm
oil on panel

Red Head I
2003
23 × 10.5 cm
oil on panel

*Head on Plinth
(Stitched Time) I*
2003
10.9 × 10.4 cm
oil on panel

Partou Zia
Entering the Visionary Zone

Dr Virginia Button

'The Imagination is not a state: it is the Human Existence itself'[1]

In more ways than one, Partou Zia defies easy categorisation. Of Persian origin – her family emigrated in 1970 – she settled in Newlyn in 1993. Her interest lies in excavating a personal, visionary landscape of cryptic meanings and dream-like imagery. Through painting, drawing and writing, her aim is to somehow represent what she perceives as the poetic experience of life, from a feminine perspective. Although this type of painting has antecedents, it is not traditionally associated with Cornwall, which has in the past seduced artists with its natural beauty. Yet the south-west tip of England has played an important role for Partou as an artist. Having felt increasingly swamped by the visual overload of the metropolis, she has now found in this relatively remote part of the country, a place conducive to solitude and reflection that allows her imagination to breathe.

Partou's approach to painting, by its very nature, discourages reductive interpretation. Just as the artist herself resists over-working the material of paint, to avoid 'closing it down', any interpretation of her work needs to be cautious of over-explication. What follows in this short introductory essay are some thoughts on her aims as painter, and some indication of the significance of her residency at St Ives to the development of her recent work.

1. The Four Zoas – Aspects of the Self

Under the terms of the residency, Partou Zia was invited to respond to the work of an artist represented in Tate's Collection. At a decisive point in her development as a painter, the work of William Blake (1757–1827), in particular his first epic poem *Vala* (1797) – or, as known in its final version, *The Four Zoas, The Torments of Love & Jealousy in the Death & Judgement of Albion & the Ancient Man* (c.1797–1807), coalesced with existing interests, and encouraged her to take a pivotal leap towards realizing her aims.

The work of this visionary poet and artist is notoriously impenetrable. A vehicle for his personal interpretation of Christian belief and the meaning of existence, it brings together an exhaustive range of modern and ancient sources and esoteric texts. In an age of enlightenment, Blake gave voice to the irrational, and celebrated the power of the imagination. *Vala* or *The Four Zoas*, which explored the subject of the Fall of Man, was Blake's first epic poem. Apparently originating in a dream, the manuscript of Vala graphically illustrates the dizzying energy of Blake's visionary creative process, which he described himself as, 'immediate Dictation twelve or sometimes twenty or thirty lines at a time, without Premeditation and even against my will'[3]

'Being able to imagine or conjure up a spiritual world extends your boundaries and gives you the power to survive the difficulties of life and perhaps the courage to do other things'[2]

Blake regarded the Fall as a state in which the self had become divided. Man's subsequent torpor allowed his Four Zoas, or divided aspects of the self, to fight among themselves. For Blake, man can only revive, or be resurrected, when the Zoas are reunited. Vala, the nature goddess or mother of all, is the female counterpart, or emanation of Luvah, the Zoa who represents passion. In *Vala*, the first version of Blake's poem, Luvah sends Vala to seduce Urizen, or reason, and their dominion over him contributes to man's Fall.

Blake later described the Four Zoas as Urizen [reason], Luvah [emotion], Urthona [imagination] and Tharmas [body]. Each Zoa had an emanation, a term used in the eighteenth century to describe a spiritual essence, though, as Robin Hamlyn has pointed out, Blake's emanations assume a more concrete form, almost always female. Separated from their male counterparts, these female emanations are reminiscent of Eve, whose creation out of Adam precedes the Fall of Man. In Blakean terms, the separation of man from his female counterpart precipitates the split of man's personality. Without his emanation, man's rational Zoa takes control.[4]

For Partou, *The Four Zoas* is about finding unity after the expulsion from the Garden of Eden, 'not a Christian sense of unity, but a sensuous, joyous, nature-driven unity'. She has noted a similar idea of the split personality in the writings of Jung, who subdivided personality into the four categories of sensation, thinking, feeling and intuition. For Jung, thinking is opposed to feeling and sensation to intuition, and the dominance of one of these categories in an individual helps to explain neurosis.[5]

In her new paintings, the artist has given herself license to enter the visionary zone, to tap into her unconscious, allowing buried thoughts, feelings and memories to take shape on canvases larger than her own studio had previously allowed. Blake's unorthodox and haunting account of the divided self has enriched her own exploration of the intuitive, irrational aspects of experience, and search for self-knowledge.

2. Search for the Self

Partou regards her artistic practice as her route or 'tunnel' to self-knowledge. It is a burning, dedicated quest, the kind that underpins almost all mystical thought. But this quest has by no means led her into a state of suffocating self-absorption. She has a searching intellect and a voracious appetite for books and ideas. Partou is herself an accomplished writer, an author of short plays and a journal. Her approach to her work – indeed her way of thinking and feeling about the world – is informed not just by other artists, but by a pantheon of philosophers, ancient and modern, critical theorists, feminists, psychologists – in fact by any text that might give clues to the meaning of existence, from such sacred works as the *Bhagvad Gita* (dating between 2nd century BC and 2000 AD), to the poems of W B Yeats, and writings of Maurice Blanchot, Martin Heidegger, and Luce Irigaray.

'My project is an ontological one. Everything I write, paint, draw and make is enfolded in the impending answer to my incessant rhetoric of: "who/what is the I?"'[6]

This desire to experience and understand the inexplicable has its roots in childhood. She was born in Tehran into a family of left-wing political activists. Her father, a doctrinaire communist, frowned on all religious activity or inclination, and blocked any nascent artistic ambitions. Ironically, this rigorous ideological background supplied the mental tools with which to assimilate philosophical systems and religious thought: 'I only had a ticket to communism, and in a way that was my ticket to critical reading, because communism is a dialectical, objective way of thinking. And it gave me permission to enter a world of which I wasn't a member'.

The world Partou refers to is not only the abstract world of religious ideas, but, in more concrete terms, the world into which she was suddenly propelled aged eleven. As a Persian émigré in London, other children undoubtedly found her exotic, but in ways she found demeaning and alienating. To a degree, her pursuit of self-knowledge, though in itself fuelled by a perpetual unknowing, was shaped by a formative sense of displacement, of otherness.

Eager, perhaps, to acclimatise to this new environment, Partou embraced western culture. As a graduate in art history from the University of Warwick, and painting from the Slade School of Fine Art, with its prestigious tradition of figurative painting, she soaked up the conventions of western art. Her interest in spirituality later led her to the work of such early twentieth-century abstract artists as Kandinsky and Klee, who had explored the spiritual potential of colour. But, eventually she was drawn back to figurative painting, and more importantly, to her love of poetry and writing as a source of inspiration, a love first instilled by her paternal grandmother, who had read to her Persia's traditional epic poems.

Until the end of 2002, Partou remained ostensibly tied to conventional subjects, exploring the traditional genres of the domestic interior and the self-portrait. The transformation of her work through poetic imagination has been a gradual process, which has evolved unmistakably during her residency.

3. The Self-Portrait as the Beloved

Partou's series of self-portraits completed between 1998 and 2001, may be seen as a strategy to assert an identity for herself, as both a woman and a painter. Typically, she is shown in the act of painting, her naked figure shamelessly filling the canvas. Superficially, it might appear that – like a number of other modern women artists – she was aiming to invert the objectification of the female form by a predominantly male culture, to change the passive female muse into the active protagonist, in control of her body and her creativity. Yet, in the context of Partou's quest for self-

*Writing in
My Blue Book*
2002
120 × 94 cm
oil on canvas

knowledge, her intention can be read in a slightly different light, as part of a search for spiritual wholeness: 'My focus or the true genre is to seek the wholeness of body and psyche, as potential in the 'I' who is both woman and painter'[7].

In work made during the residency, the self-portraiture has given way to depictions of an alter ego, first painted in red, then green and more recently golden yellow. Of asexual appearance, and always with her back turned to the viewer – drawing attention to a spine, strangely configured by the number eight, the symbol of infinity – her identity remains enigmatic and undisclosed. In these pictures, the alter ego appears to direct, caress or protect a pair of lovers. Gradually, she has dematerialised, becoming a shadowy presence, perhaps reflecting the formal and metaphorical completion of her role.

A clue to the identity of this figure lies in the Sufic idea of the Beloved. In Sufism, the mystical branch of Islam, the Beloved is an emblem of the true self, the unknown self, the self united with God. Perhaps this alter ego is Partou's Beloved, her higher self? She has written: 'Who is the one-that-is-not-I? It seems fairly plausible to regard the creative echo as that of the mystic's beloved, which is often represented as an idealized representation of a better self, in the name of a greater religious other, to whom the ascetic or visionary would submit, and be subsumed in the passionate folds of divine love'[8].

In Time's Relief
2003
180 × 200 cm
oil on canvas

The theme of love has emerged strongly in Partou's recent work. It is difficult not to link her rapturous, sensual, yet tender images of lovers, as they sleep, embrace or comfort one another, with the Sufi's burning love of and yearning for union with God.

4. The Specific and the Momentary

Memory has always fascinated Partou. In earlier works, the representation of the familiar space of the studio, and the domestic interiors of her cottage in Newlyn, allowed her to explore feelings of loss and absence. Her family's departure from Iran took place under the guise of a holiday. She left her bedroom containing all its childhood treasures, unaware that she would never return: 'As a child, not to go back to what you've left means that there is always the possibility that it still exists somewhere in the ether…And that's how the interiors began to take shape. I explored that feeling through them'.

Through these pictures she was also striving to achieve a sense of reality that extended beyond the realm of representation. As she writes: 'The aim is to make of the (presumed) "empty" space, or the unremarkable objects around me, something other than mere sensory information. It is an attempt at vivifying space through the energy of presence'[9].

Lost Equations
2003
180 × 200 cm
oil on canvas

The Green Stairs
2001
206 × 99 cm
oil on canvas

In these paintings she began to pursue an elusive moment, the 'poetic zone', a 'moment of being'.[10] So memory, both personal and collective, contribute to this experience of the present moment, as she explains: 'More than anything, the paintings that I'm doing now are about the idea of the complexity of memory and the presence of being here…You are doing something now, and it's quite sensation-based, but there's a cerebral aspect to memory that is taking you somewhere else, and yet, it's connected to the now. So it's a kind of cubistic approach to the now'[11].

Although the series of interiors and self-portraits accomplished technical sophistication and a certain vivacity, the experience of the momentary remained elusive. The subject matter prolonged Partou's dependence on specific spaces. For example, in *The Green Stairs* (2001), despite the vertiginous depiction of space as felt, the composition dictates a specific and recognisable point of entry for the viewer, poised at the top of staircase. Drawing on unconscious thought for their subjects, the recent paintings dispense with any such certainty.

Partou's move towards imaginative, dream-like subject matter is marked by *Owl Vision* (2003), in which she first introduced the motif of lovers. An owl, traditionally associated with wisdom and insight, hovers at a window. Inside the lovers take refuge, veiled from the outside world by a billowing curtain. In her pictures curtains function as a framing device, separating internal and external spaces, providing a source of movement or drama. Curtains, like veils, reveal and conceal. Like the chalice she depicts in another work, they suggest an invitation to partake of something, a desire to discover what lies beyond. Conversely, they might also point to the artist's wish to keep the unconscious meanings of her work under wraps.

This new freedom in terms of subject matter has been matched by a less controlled approach to the medium of paint. Her desire to experience the momentary has led Partou to the technique of

Owl Vision
2003
157 × 183 cm
oil on canvas

drawing with paint, in search of a fluency akin to that which the American painter Phillip Guston achieved in his mature style. In the late 1960s Guston wrote: 'It is the bareness of drawing I like. The act of drawing is what locates, what suggests, discovers. At times it seems enough to draw, without having the distraction of colour and mass. Yet it is an old ambition to make drawing and painting one'[12].

In *Reed Hall* (2002), made just before the start of her residency, Partou began to give drawing a more prominent role in her picture-making. In this image of a bleak interior, comprising a curtain, TV set and light, she began to use paint as line against areas of colour. More recently she has ceased to use drawing as a preparation for her paintings. This prompts her to work with the freedom normally associated with drawing itself, and represents a letting go of intellectual thought, and conventional rules of picture-making.

In tandem with her larger paintings, Partou has also produced a series of much smaller works on panel. Depicting such favoured themes as lovers sleeping, birds and books. These tiny, icon-like works have the kind of intensity reminiscent of such contemporary figure painters as Leon Kossoff. Although these works do not function as studies in a conventional sense, for the artist they have provided a means of 'unlocking knots', of 'opening up difficult areas of larger paintings'.

A further development can be seen in Partou's radically different approach to colour. Greens, blues, murky browns and off-whites have given way to a more strident palette, emancipated from the world of representation. She has commented: 'I'm using colour for what it is now, which is something I've always wanted to do. For example, in earlier works, such as *The Green Stairs* (2001), I painted the staircase green, because in my cottage the staircase is green…But to paint an imaginative world in strong colours is another step for me, because it's not a specific place I'm replicating – it's an interior colour, an interior world'.

The revelation of this interior world has been a baffling and sometimes painful experience for the artist. For example, the recurring clusters of eyes, which represent being looked at, but not being seen, have the uncanny quality of Blake's eyes of God in *Beatrice Addressing Dante from the Car* (1824–27) one of his best-known illustrations to Dante's *The Divine Comedy*. In another work, *Lost Equations* (2003) a classical sculpture of a woman's head on a plinth is accompanied by dead faces, one seemingly buried under a tree, others as ethereally sketched portraits. A vivid, orange-coloured book lies under a tree, its cover inscribed with a mathematical equation. The artist's love of numbers and their complexity is confounded by what she describes as her innumeracy; a failing perhaps traceable to an incident in her childhood when she failed to remember her times tables. Thus, for Partou, maths and numbers speak a beautiful language that remains mysterious.

William Blake
Beatrice Addressing Dante from the Car
1824–27
37 × 53 cm
pen and ink and watercolour on paper
Tate

In these recent paintings, fragments of ancient sculpture refer to history, and perhaps more specifically to deep-seated memories of Partou's own cultural heritage. Often they seem too vast for the canvas to contain: only the feet and ankles of one statue are visible, while another is dominated by a mere segment of a column. Such images, together with the recurring motif of gloves, suggest the monumentality of past human achievement, and memorialise the unknown artisans, who laboured to create the marvels of antiquity.

Sleeping Lovers
2003
61 × 61 cm
oil on canvas

Red Book of Dreams
2003
44 × 61 cm
oil on canvas

5. The Silent Image

While it is tempting to try to decipher Partou's almost surreal configurations of motifs in psychoanalytic terms, or by reference to her specific cultural identity, trying to explain them would undermine their magic. Although she would like the works to have some effect in the world, for Partou they are ultimately personal explorations: 'In a way the paintings themselves must remain locked mysteries – they have to – otherwise they won't work, otherwise they are playing to an audience'. Occasionally, she appears to remind the viewer, perhaps unconsciously, of the importance of not stating too much openly. In two of her most impressive works, completed in August 2003, the motif of stitched thread is conveyed by aggressive marks scratched into the paint, inferring that the meaning of the canvas is closed up.[13]

One of the hallmarks of our culture is the remorseless drive to explain everything, to reduce mysteries to tidy formulae. Despite the often altruistic purpose of this compulsion, perhaps it needs to be admitted that art should sometimes have the freedom to remain obscure, to exist on its own terms. Like Blake's poetry, Partou's recent work draws on a heady mix of the esoteric and the everyday to create a unique imaginative space, a space that resists reductive explanation, yet is rich with exploratory possibilities for both artist and viewer.

Blue Suitcase
2003
76 × 102 cm
oil on canvas

Notes

1 William Blake, *Milton: A Poem in 2 Books*, plate e, line 32.

2 Partou Zia, July 2003. Unless otherwise stated, all quotations by the artist are from conversations with the author, 25 July and 12 August 2003.

3 Letter to Butts, 25 April 1803, E729, cited in Robin Hamlyn and Michael Phillips, *William Blake*, Tate, 2000, p 274.

4 ibid., Hamlyn, p 244.

5 Anthony Storr, *Jung*, Fontana Modern Masters, 1973, 1995 edition, p 76.

6 Partou Zia, *Poetic Anatomy of the Numinous: Creative Passages into the Self as Beloved*, unpublished PhD thesis, Falmouth College of Arts, University of Plymouth, 2001, p 13.

7 Ibid, pp 92–3.

8 Ibid, p 24.

9 Ibid, p 13.

10 Ibid, p 10.

11 The idea of the 'momentary' as a full realization of the present is found in such religious practices as Buddhist or yogic meditation, or Sufism's swirling dance, and suggests a yearning for the Infinite. For Partou, the importance of memory, of tapping into the unconscious, also resonates with Jung's view that the unconscious is the single source of religious experience.

12 Quoted by Robert Storr, *Guston*, Modern Masters, Abbeville Press, 1986, p 113.

13 Partou was later appalled by news reports of an Iranian refugee in Britain who had stitched up his eyelids and lips to protest against the plight of asylum seekers. This she felt drew a correlation, albeit a painful one between her own mark making, and the horror of being closed-up, of being silenced.

The Sleep of Hands
2003
180 × 200 cm
oil on canvas

Partou Zia

Biography

Biography

1958	Born Tehran Persia
1970	Emigrated to England
1977–1980	University of Warwick, BA Hons Art History
1986–1991	Slade School of Fine Art, BA Hons Fine Art
1993	Moved to Cornwall
1998–2001	PhD Falmouth College of Arts & University of Plymouth

Solo Exhibitions

2003	Tate St Ives
2002	Art Space Gallery, London
2000	Art Space Gallery, London
	Plymouth Arts Centre
1999	Royal Cornwall Museum, Truro
1998	Newlyn Art Gallery
1997	Thornton-Bevan Arts, London

Group Exhibitions

1999	*Four Young Artists*, Art Space, London
1998	*In/Sight*, Exeter University
1997	*Gallery Artists I*, Reed's Wharf Gallery, London

1997	*A Sense of Place*, Collyer Bristow Gallery, London
1996	*Landscapes from Penwith*, Hastings Museum and Gallery
1996–1999	*Spring Open*, Connaught Brown, London
1995	*John Moores Exhibition 19*, Walker Art Gallery, Liverpool
1994	*Response to Landscape*, Beatrice Royal Gallery, Southampton
1993	Salthouse Gallery, St Ives, London
1992	Carpenters Road Studios, London
1990	*Works on Paper*, The Boundary Gallery, London
1989	*Young Contemporaries*, Whitworth Gallery, Manchester

Awards/Residencies

2003	Tate St Ives Artist in Residence, Porthmeor Studios (March–Sept)
2003	Arts Council of England, South West, decibel
2003	Creative Skills Consortium
2003	Arts Council, South West Travel Grant
2001	South West Arts Artist's Award

Collections

British Museum, London

Private Collections

This catalogue has been published to accompany the exhibition
Partou Zia *Entering the Visionary Zone*, resulting from the first Tate St Ives
Artist Residency at the historic Porthmeor Studios.

25 October 2003 – 25 January 2004

Essay by Dr Virginia Button

ISBN 1 85437 527 X

A catalogue record for this publication is available from the British Library

Editors Susan Daniel-McElroy and Sara Hughes
Photography Bob Berry
Design Groundwork, Skipton
Repro and Print Triangle, Leeds

This project has been made possible by funding from the following organisations:
Esmee Fairbairn Foundation | Arts Council of England, South West | decibel | Tate Members
Creative Skills Consortium | Falmouth College of Arts

Partou Zia is currently represented by Art Space Gallery: www.artspacegallery.co.uk